THE

SERIES

Series Titles

Happy Everything
Caitlin Cowan

Dear Lo
Brady Bove

Sadness of the Apex Predator
Dion O'Reilly

The Trouble With Being a Childless Only Child
Michelle Meyer

Don't Feed the Animal
Hikari Miya

Glitter City
Bonnie Jill Emanuel

Listening to Mars
Sally Ashton

The Watching Sky
Judy Brackett Crowe

Let It Be Told in a Single Breath
Russell Thorburn

The Blue Divide
Linda Nemec Foster

Lake, River, Mountain
Mark B. Hamilton

Talking Diamonds
Linda Nemec Foster

Poetic People Power
Tara Bracco (ed.)

The Green Vault Heist
David Salner

There is a Corner of Someplace Else
Camden Michael Jones

Everything Waits
Jonathan Graham

We Are Reckless
Christy Prahl

Always a Body
Molly Fuller

Bowed As If Laden With Snow
Megan Wildhood

Silent Letter
Gail Hanlon

New Wilderness
Jenifer DeBellis

Fulgurite
Catherine Kyle

The Body Is Burden and Delight
Sharon White

Bone Country
Linda Nemec Foster

Not Just the Fire
R.B. Simon

Monarch
Heather Bourbeau

The Walk to Cefalù
Lynne Viti

Praise for

Happy Everything

"Caitlin Cowan has written the kind of book women poets were once warned against. Plathian in its ferocious truth-telling, it refuses to be shushed, spinning narratives of cheating fathers and husbands, of men with 'rabbit-rattlesnake / risotto' on their breath. Cowan brilliantly frames the poems via epigraphs from a cooking and etiquette manual, and offers a sequence of prose poems titled after relics of material culture, as in '*Leifheit Perle* Handheld Crumb Sweeper,' in which the crumber is 'a tiny metal cog in / a creaking old machine, an industry as old as I do.' The underlying reality of the book is the excruciating ache of containment in that creaking machine, and the lyric mode as a powerful mechanism of liberation."

—Diane Seuss
author of *frank: sonnets*
winner of the Pulitzer Prize

"Caitlin Cowan's *Happy Everything* takes on birthdays, anniversaries, Easter, Mother's Day, the New Year, Halloween— all the markers that insist upon celebration, whether or not the speaker feels joy. *Happy Everything* is the antidote to Hallmark cards, to the Hallmark channel, to forced gaiety as it is thrust upon women to perform happiness and beauty no matter their real life events. Cowan subverts what we think we know about marriage and divorce and the traumas of childhood in a witty, heartbreaking voice all her own. This is a terrific debut!"

—Denise Duhamel
author of *Second Story*

"Caitlin Cowan's debut collection is a celebration against obligation, an origin story of gendered half-truths, and an entreaty toward reclamation, that we may be the 'unruly golden dog' of our own damn stories. Pulsing with a deft balance of wisdom and righteous rage, the masterful, lyrical, and gut-punching poems of *Happy Everything* look the staid picture of domestic 'happiness' square in the face and say, for all our sakes, 'not good enough.' Punctuated by etiquette manuals and frivolous objects of housewifery, Cowan saws through the harmful messaging of compulsory heterosexuality in an era-defying dialogue with our foremothers of poetry, diving into the wreck and towing us toward 'the truth's frigid / tide.' Evoking Adrienne Rich, Dorianne Laux, and, of course, Plath's 'Daddy,' Cowan writes of the dangers of 'the wrong wedding': 'Though I will not see my father / again, I will look for him in other men.' The speaker of this book and her mother, in their own ways, know better: 'When [Mama] told me I wouldn't die from this, I listened.' Cowan's poems sear with wit, precision, and a steadfast allegiance to the underground sisterhood that keeps us human: 'the kind who are loved without labor.' In one of the book's several nods to *Little Women*, the speaker dreams she is a bedridden Beth, but indeed Caitlin Cowan is Jo, most ardently Jo, penning her 'narrative incoherence' into unforgettable verse. *Happy Everything*, I wish every lucky reader who opens this brilliant book for the first time."

—Jenny Molberg
author of *The Court of No Record*

"What a rare and welcome surprise it is to come upon a young poet who possesses enough ambition and talent to illuminate—unforgettably, I think, in the case of Caitlin Cowan—what might be called *the too muchness of life*, to celebrate that nameless mortal abundance variously ending in ecstasy, despair, hope, grief, prayer, emotional collapse, or silent acceptance. Cowan is very much a visual poet, and the uncanny, brilliantly diverse quality of her imagery and tropes lights the path to both wisdom and hilarity. Her language is rich and often deeply witty, seducing the reader into the poem's embrace, its song of life, a life fully lived on at least eleven different levels. I passionately recommend *Happy Everything* to any member of the human species who somehow missed the train and hungers to know exactly what it is like to live on planet Earth."

—B. H. Fairchild
author of *An Ordinary Life*

"At the center of *Happy Everything* lies a stunning examination of what could too easily be dismissed as a 'failed marriage,' brought vividly into focus by Caitlin Cowan's uncommon gift for rendering even the bleakest scenes with lush particularity and eviscerating wit. In hindsight, it's hard not to see everything as metaphor, from a handheld crumb sweeper to a set of champagne flutes to 'the untamed woman sewn into a dress / that didn't fit.' But these would-be talismans gesture toward something larger: Cowan's fierce, ironic reckoning with one of our most entrenched institutions, one that is itself 'a mere oar // that slaps the sea's wild chop.' As much as this book serves as a kind of post-mortem, it is also an assertion of selfhood, an act of reclamation."

—Mark Bibbins
author of *13th Balloon*

"In her powerful first volume of poems, *Happy Everything*, Caitlin Cowan explores, with unflinching honesty and heartbreak, a gendered expectation to serve the pleasures of men, to seek, in reply, a more sustainable version of joy and reach, in turn, a deeper understanding of love. In a domestic sphere where food provides both symbol and example of care, the poet refuses an easy dismissal of the beauty and generosities forged there, but rather authenticates an attendant complexity of affections fraught with loneliness and betrayal of oneself and others. We hear, with its poignancy of detail and emotional precision, the voice of a fully mature narrative lyricist, rooted in dailiness and yet keen to intensify our gaze with an abiding sense of artistry and wisdom. A deeply moving collection."

—Bruce Bond
author of *Patmos*

"Reading *Happy Everything* by Caitlin Cowan is to feel the crush of a champagne-flute cage match between Iggy Pop and Anne Sexton set amidst a bachelorette fight club in some rusted-out Detroit tool and die shop. This is a book of fierce intelligence, formal mastery, and a wide-open heart, in which a woman fights to claim her art, her power, and herself from the vampirism of social expectations and forced self-deprecations that want her to believe 'sugar and silence were the same thing,' where one is expected 'to admire / the untamed woman sewn into a dress / that didn't fit.' Out of the rubble of a fraught youth and a bad marriage emerges a voice that is 'not content to be mere / decoration, mere idea.' I've been waiting for this poet's first book for a long time. I am left gutted by its brilliance, by its brakelines and linebreaks, by its manifolds and musicality, by its movement between demolition and rebirth, and by the healing it flowers forth."

—Matt W. Miller
author of *Tender the River*

HAPPY EVERYTHING

POEMS

CAITLIN COWAN

CORNERSTONE PRESS

UNIVERSITY OF WISCONSIN-STEVENS POINT

Cornerstone Press, Stevens Point, Wisconsin 54481
Copyright © 2024 Caitlin Cowan
www.uwsp.edu/cornerstone

Printed in the United States of America by
Point Print and Design Studio, Stevens Point, Wisconsin

Library of Congress Control Number: 2023950560
ISBN: 978-1-960329-22-6

Cover design by David Wojciechowski | www.davidwojo.com
Cover art © Sarah J. Sloat

Cornerstone Press titles are produced in courses and internships offered by the
Department of English at the University of Wisconsin–Stevens Point.

DIRECTOR & PUBLISHER
Dr. Ross K. Tangedal

EXECUTIVE EDITORS
Jeff Snowbarger, Freesia McKee

EDITORIAL DIRECTOR
Ellie Atkinson

SENIOR EDITORS
Brett Hill, Grace Dahl

PRESS STAFF
Carolyn Czerwinski, Sophie McPherson, Natalie Reiter, Ava Willett

For Matilda—

May you sit wherever, however, and with whomever you please.

POEMS

III.

IV.

V.

"You haven't heard what I wanted to tell you. Sit down and listen; for indeed I want to do right, and make you happy," she said, hoping to soothe him with a little reason,—which proved that she knew nothing about love.

—*Little Women*

Happy Everything

In Mama's nightmare, she's young again.
Her wedding unfolds at the local

McDonald's—the groom is her youngest brother,
who carves a wizened pumpkin and mutters

his snot-nosed vows. Christmas lights spatter
the walls like buckshot. Her guests ransack

cornucopias and tear at glittered valentines—
they soap the windows: *Happy Everything.*

So much to celebrate: here is Mama's horror.
She the decorator, the spiker of punches

and curler of ribbons. But when her hands petrify
into gloves of pain, it is not a dream.

The part where the parties end, where her husband
leaves and takes the guests, is not,

alas, the dream. She writes toasts for parlor ghosts
but thinks this is absurd: all the year's eruptions

of joy and *hello* stuffed in one
dumb night. The terror is the awful party

inside the party—the one where no one's left.
It's not the lost house she fears, or its dining room

ablaze with brandy, the windows fogged
with a turkey's steam. Instead she sweats

through the night under the threat
of unlicked invitations, missed buttons

at wedding feasts. Her bad dreams
are the sounds of no one

in her kitchen, neighbors potlucking
on her rotten deck, silent and swirling

their sangria, wishing its whirlpool
would drown them. When I told her

my young marriage was over, we were awake.
She could still taste the envelopes on her tongue.

I.

"When a man and woman eat together … it is proper for the man to lead the way to the dining room in a strange place or, if it is familiar ground, for them to walk to the door together."

—*Practical Cookery and the Etiquette and Service of the Table: A Compilation of Principles of Cookery and Recipes with Suggestions for Etiquette for Various Occasions*

Half Past

The blow to the head clangs like a lens flare, shines like a big bronze knell. After impact comes agnosia—my father asked his patients to sketch the time. What came out were half clocks, six numbers only or twelve teeming on one side: *visual neglect.* These were their wholes. Some claimed their left legs were not their own, others had ignored their right hands, fallow with disuse. At night

I conjured the man who shaved half his face, the hungry woman who didn't see the right side of her plate, the girl whose blush pinked just one (which?) of her cheeks. Face half-mown, belly half-caved, a clown who halts the whiteface halfway. My father's dictations murmured under the door: ticker tape run off its reel. *Unilateral neglect*—a glitch in the system, the mechanisms meant to churn and bring us home. Encode, store, retrieve. I know I can. Encode the night the secretary knock-

knocked, dripping with rain on the doorstep, delivering mail that could have waited. Store what you pulled from his suit coat one morning (what was it?) and how you guiltily put it back. When my father asked a patient to draw his first car, his old cat, his wife's face, just half rose up from the ink. *The memory is whole, but simply being ignored.* Retrieve the final afternoon, half

the bedroom closet gone, half the shoes sauntered off (had he left the slippers?), half the nightstand stripped of coins. Half hallucination, half memory, half dream of certainty. *Neglect of the body, the space around it, the places beyond its reach.* Among the papers he left, gulls at rest on shore, a file on the blotter flayed open—there, half tulips standing sentry before a graphite sea.

Happy Easter

The other woman's name on my tongue, rising
      like ruin, like a certain cat:
            alive and dead behind a rolled stone.

While the other woman's car
      sleeps in the street, vengeance
            stings its way up my throat—

the shiv of a key glints between my knuckles.
      No ma'am, I won't lacerate
            the white skin of the other woman's Caprice

the way Mama once taught me to abrade my cheating
      Daddy's blue Yukon. I can resurrect his face
            if I roll my eyes back in my head

and squint through the keyhole into the room
      where I keep the things that can't come back:
            men and marriage and Jesus.

I can't be Mama's kind of woman
      who mistakes a scar for the heart's own healing.
            Take that, the key said as it flashed

across Daddy's passenger side. *Just like that*, Mama said.
      God damn… that's dark, my lover says now—
            the key blooms in my palm like a kiss.

Folie à Famille

"Antonovsky suggests, as Freud did, that
psychological illness is born of narrative
incoherence, a life story veering off course."
—Rachel Aviv, *The New Yorker*, April 2017

I spent the whole session balloon-lettering FUCK YOU onto
a yellow legal pad. I had been mum for weeks, and the men
in the room were rapt. *She's writing us a message*, one said.
And boy, was I ever. The dust motes haloed my head while I
scrawled my holy writ. Another time Mama slipped a tape
recorder into my pocket. *It's not fair*, she said, showing me
how to use it, *two big men ganging up on a little girl*. I had,
of course, used it before to record the dumb story of my
young life. I could feel it in my pocket during those long
weeks, heavy as Daddy's big textbooks. At night I'd creep
from bed and scan the words for broken: *aphasia, agnosia,
amnesia*. Afterwards she'd listen to every word, cluck her
tongue, and wind the tape back up into a waiting asp. These
were the days when I still knew every part of the story. They
met, they had me, we were we. One time I spent the whole
session with my eyes closed. I saw dangerous weather-map
hues though my hands weren't pressing my lids. I never
knew whether I was well or ill, dreamed of being bedridden
like Beth with no Jo there to help her die. We were not
sick but simple, believed there were still threads tying us,
still more rungs on a ladder that would lift us. The last time
I ran from the musty office and leapt on the hood of his
Yukon. I clambered to its pollen-dusted roof and sat there,
took root like a lotus: tendrils searching the depths. I had
no plan other than *make it stop*. Those two big men stood
there dumbstruck, in awe of me. *I think she's trying to make a
statement*, one said. *She's lost it*, said the other. One of those
men was a doctor. One of those men was my father.

Happy Father's Day

How to crook a pinball, how to lose
at chess. Daddy taught me

how to air guitar and drum
the back headrest. Cars

he wasn't much for—
that was Granddad's thing—so

Daddy wasn't there
when I learned to brake

that spring. But I learned
the word *malingering*:

making up your pain.
Daddy said his patients

did it almost every day.
Did I make this up,

I thought, the night
that I came home

and found a pot of early peas
pebbled on the floor.

Does this really hurt,
I thought, thumbing

broken plates, or is this feeling
just a hungry fake?

I was quiet as I swept
the shards into the trash,

silent as the *shush* the man
I married fed me with.

Try to stop
without a stutter, try

to stop without a sound.
That's the trick that Granddad

taught me: how the rubber
kissed the ground.

Eating Alone

A man ate breakfast at work. Every morning for 35 years Dal asked my grandfather if he wanted some cereal before shift. *J'eat jet?* he'd say. And every morning for 35 years my grandfather said, *Yeah, I'm ok.* Each day the same. The story is one I know well. Dal ate alone in that bald break room day after decade: it took grit. Like sugar, solitude can't sustain us.

A man who eats breakfast at work has no one to eat with. Dal died ages ago, and this is what my grandfather regrets: never sharing Frosted Flakes with him on a single Motor City morning. *J'eat jet?* This is his pain. *All set, today.* He clocked in, let Dal's offer pass over him, a benediction, then set to work on something like six thousand sterile mornings—the taste of engine oil on his tongue. In college, I hear it, like spoiled cream, in my professor's mouth: *j'eat jet*, a prime example of Midwest elision. I can taste its linguistics even now.

A man eating breakfast at work ain't ashamed, hoping to bend low over a bowl of milk and wheat with the men he knows better each day. Fixing my first meal in the apartment with only my name on the lease, though I never knew him, I think of Dal as my hands tremble to lift a dish. I can't decide whether to rush or linger. *J'eat jet?* I say to myself. I have tried to figure out what to do with my grandfather's regret. I think I'll eat it with a spoon.

Happy Anniversary

In the dining room, I dream the plates levitate as if on wires, exposing
chewed gristle and bone; in the galley, we shout *corner* and *behind*

between secret bites of their offal. We avoid collision, eschew
contact. Sometimes the servers shorten it, *hot behind,*

to warn of warm plates we can't see. But all I think is *gee, buy me
a drink first.* With plates of pheasant and beef, they zip behind

me like strangers, though the night before we drowned in tequila
together at an industry bar. Days regular as dishes: the party vibe hindered

by actual work, the innuendo thick as roux, the bar a trench I worry
I can't escape. The plates hover like hummingbirds: maybe hindsight

is the only way I'll see it—the soused husbands and new couples peering
through their empty glasses, making me small. Some CEO pats my behind

and asks for another glass of wine. I can smell the rabbit-rattlesnake risotto on his breath, see the glinting band on his finger. They're behind

me now, the nights I came home smelling of smoke: Wagyu for the guests and American Spirit for me, goal-weight starving, lighting up behind

a dumpster while the patio winked citronella. Oh, the glitter of brandied laughter. Outside, I fingered pennies for the wrong wedding: a final fixture to hide behind.

Self-Portrait as Maillard Reaction

When I linger over the stove's concentric fire, I remember
the first burgers I made in your filthy bachelor's kitchen. I held
the heft of beef like a brick; it ached for a window to slaughter.
Raw hands deep in the raw meat, I broke it into four pieces,
then rubbed each hunk's edges smooth. The mud-colored
patties—alight on chintzy buns—still bore the marks
of a grinder: wormy tracks in their midst, the paths of maggots
through a body. But I got better at cooking, better at forgetting
the shackle of dinners on the table at five. Helpless
husband, marzipan prince in your father's suit: you
never knew how you grew up or whether. Think of the night
you called me to ask how to brown the beef yourself. At thirty
you didn't know a thing about cooking, so I paused a conversation
at a dinner five states away. I should have told you
helpless things do not eat, but are eaten. Instead I froze
beneath a streetlamp, tried to describe the thaw
of pink beef going brown as autumn leaves. And why
wouldn't I: at home, *that smells good* was the only compliment
I'd get in a week, or a month—our little horseshoe kitchen
a court I held sway over. The way to a man's heart and all that.
Then I let you go. You let me go. And now I'm struck
anew by Mama's advice about browning beef: she warned
that just because it looked ready didn't mean it was.
If you're patient, all that heat makes something delicious, but
it's hard to wait when you're starved. Dear, foolish man:
I was still pink inside. But I was so proud of that terrible meal.
We ate it, gray and bland, and I cooked a thousand more.

Happy Birthday

I don't remember what our *special breakfast* was. The last square photo I have of him is of his hand, wearing a cheap ring that says I KNOW. Mine said I LOVE YOU—I bought the set at Spencer's for ten bucks. His wedding ring didn't fit him anymore: he'd put on too much weight. I had too. I don't know my ring size, now or then. Was it turkey sausage and cheddar cheese? On toast? His smile is smaller in each picture, the LOVE OF MY LIFE captions phonier and phonier until they stop altogether. Were there more photos of cocktails than photos of the cat before or after I kissed another man? I left the cat with him: a furry consolation prize he cherished more deeply than me. There are still photos of cats, but they are other cats. One of them is mine. He would have loved her. But again, loved her more than me. It was an English muffin. He loved to create new dishes that required no knowledge of cooking, a facet of his personality wholly unappealing to me. But he would bring it to me in bed, two buttered English muffins topped with circles of turkey sausage, each island covered in square flaps of cheddar cheese, salt and pepper sprinkled right on their greasy, orangey sheen. I was with him for exactly one third of my birthdays—the ratio recedes, but slowly. The whole thing was microwaved into a mush I ate on special occasions like today, or whenever I was half-dead and loved him, whenever I was hungover and loved him, whenever I was hurt and loved him, which was almost, bless us, all the time.

My Father Drives to Muskegon
with a Bouquet of Flowers

only to be refused by his only child.
That hard summer sparkled
darkly: sweat at the small of his back
as he sped northwest. On the three-hour
drive he wondered would the mums
hold in the heat and did I know
they were my birth flower—the languages

we learn before going somewhere new.
I sawed through the summer
on the cheap violin he'd bought.
It was the year I turned fifteen, long
after he stopped coming home, had left
only spare change in his night-
stand drawer. On the last day
of camp he arrived in secret, slunk
into a rain-worn bench in the back.
Though the air hung heavy

between the lodgepole pines that flanked
the concert shell the conductor
took his time, explained the word *aleatoric*:
chaos and freedom, left up to chance—
my father could not imagine me
swimming in that confusion, and yet
I had: own echo, self-sonar, deft
as the bats that haloed our woodland chapel
that season and every season since.
The symphony was called

And God Created Great Whales.
My father remembered his own eyes

drying over the Old Testament as a boy
while he listened, remembered God
sometimes made lovely things
that we were not made to know.
He could feel my concentration—
a leviathan's shadow passing
over him like a cloud—but could only
count the minutes until it was over:
crescendo, whale song, tremolo.
After, in the sea of shrill parents

he searched for my face which
is also his face and found me.
A circle of young girls closed
around me, a pearl. And who
was he to prise open that craggy
shell, he who made a grown-up
of me so young, who couldn't love
my mother but ached
to hold my blonde locks
in his fingers, still. For years

my only inheritance
will be the comparison lobbed
in anger: *arrogant, just like him.*
Though I will not see my father
again, I will look for him in other
men, will let his absence flood me
like cold water. For now, the matter
at hand: where to shelve his mind
for the drive back down, how to rid
his brain of the zebra mussel shells
that sliced the soles of his every thought—
what to do with the flowers, the million
eager hands of its petals reaching
far enough to find nothing to hold.

What's Left of Michigan

The first time I tasted you, it was forbidden: a curse.
We were eighteen in my Mama's house, sweating coldly
to the ticking of frozen bark on maples.

Here, though Ford feeds families it also stands
for *Fucker Only Runs Downhill*, which you said so loudly
I worried she'd hear. I pressed my fingertips—still stung

from digging the car out to get you—over your smile.
Winter's skin cooled with our own as we dozed
naked, clandestine in my old brass bed. That year

the house down the street hawked cemetery blankets
and poinsettias, their prices spray-painted on plywood.
Though she silenced my swearing, Mama would hiss

shithole as we drove by, like she'd never seen the litter
of car husks flanking their lawn, the bony swingsets
with gone children. This is home: these dead streets

and this chalkboard sky, those hummocks of soiled snow
I shoveled so quickly my heart protested. Mama begged me
to lift more slowly, but I had to get out. I had to get out

when I sped past the shithole years later, this time peddling wreaths
and spaniel puppies that would drown in the freezing stream.
When I arrived I ended us, rewarded my own frigid scooping

by turning you out, pointing you home. It was, yes, cold.
I came inside and throbbed with awful heat, fetal in that same
damn bed. Mama called you *asshole, pindick, turd.*

I held her while she vomited the night that Daddy left,
so when she told me I wouldn't die from this, I listened.
She stroked my hair; the windowpanes creaked their assent.

II.

"The woman follows the waiter or hostess and the man brings up the rear. The waiter pulls out the choice seat first and the woman takes this

unless for some reason she prefers another.

Her escort sees that she is comfortably seated and then seats himself, usually taking the opposite chair … Otherwise he will probably sit at her left though

it is quite proper to sit where one desires."

—*Ibid*

Leifheit Perle Handheld Crumb Sweeper

Sweeps up crumbs, dust, spilt ashtrays. For table tops, upholstery and smooth or carpet surfaces. Three bristle brushes. Prise cover off to empty.

After dinner, a good hostess will sweep the crumbs from her table. I'd seen Mama do it many times. Run the little white box over the tablecloth, let its four wheels and long bristles fling the dross into its chambers. I used to like looking at it later, the two neat rows of dinner in miniature: a sparrow-grass scale, two caviar eyes, the dust of croque-en-bouche past. It made everything small, like memory. She sent it to me once I was married, still in its original box. Originally $15.00, she snagged it on clearance for $2.47. *Handkehrer, ramasse-miettes, handrolveger*—the little box has orders overseas. I had the good china, and I had the husband. All that was left was to keep it clean. It came with a two-year warranty: longer than the span of my marriage.

*

In times gone by the waiter would use a small broom and dustpan. This was, for most, too cumbersome, too symbolic. God forbid a man would hold housewifery in his hands. The standard metal bars were patented before the Second World War. In 1950, Ray Machine bought a patent from a Baltimore restaurateur. And in thirty years my mother would buy her Leifheit from Hudson's outside Detroit—in thirty more I would hold it here in my hands. I don't know how long I will keep its obsequious shush in my cabinet. *Someone will want it*, I think. A good crumber in the pocket of every good waiter, a ludicrous gadget in the sideboard of every ludicrous wife. They will endure as long as we make messes: as long as other people make messes of us.

*

The night he proposed, I ordered the soufflé at the French Room. But when the server lifted the cloche, there was no soufflé. Just an obscenity of flowers and a tiny red box. As small, as bloody as my heart. An old married couple bought us champagne. I can't remember its taste or any. I think he asked because he thought it was time. Had some money coming in. There was no speech. There were no reasons for his love. Just my name—first, last, and middle—rote as a phone number's drone. Between dinner and the dessert of flowers, our server scraped the table's surface, her crumber a tiny metal cog in a creaking old machine, an industry as old as *I do*. I drive by the Adolphus from time to time. I can see our table through the window from the street. We only got to ask for it once. At Christmas, you can see the city's glowing tree from your seat. To whomever is sitting there now: you are looking at its glint. I am looking at you, your crumbs. Let me make you, for a moment, pristine.

Best Order

A teacher once told me to hold a ruler like a razor

beneath my sentences—up to the jugular—a threat

to make them stranger, to see them for the first time

again and again, so I might find the flaws

and fix. As I look at you, as I have for most of the last decade,

through the bottom of my glass, through a bedsheet

of smoke, I understand—we must make each other

strange again each day. Even as the prying stars

peer in through the Venetians, we

must blind ourselves to that starshine of sameness

so we might see—vex ourselves once more

to venture a straighter line, a sentence that stabs and is kind.

Happy Halloween

I.

There are two sluts left, so one is about to die,
you say into your longneck, a microphone
for what you know. The awful mathematics
of films like these: all but one woman has to go.
We cull those we can't rein in real life
from our plots like weeds—the rising action,
our greedy ascent, is built on their bodies,
flayed open and maimed. *Just wait*, you mutter.
You swig your beer. I wonder who you are.

II.

These guts, these knife thrusts,
these slugs exploding like supernovas
from unsuspecting chests—they're all still here
in high resolution, grey matter so gelatinous
it throbs with thought; saliva so sticky
we taste the tide. I've returned to childhood,
cloaked in the basement's pall, gorging
on film after unrated film because Mama
thought *unrated* meant the same as *safe*.
She did not know that no eyes,
no ratings board stuffed with clergy
or censors had ever seen the horror
gurgling in those old cassettes.
There is no safety. That is horror.

III.

Reveling in imagined superiority—
you don't have enough bullets,
you ass—we list wisdom: *the camera*
will survive, but the cameraman will not.
If you enter the spirit realm,
make sure you have an exit strategy.
The call is absolutely
coming from inside the house.
Why do we make them this way,
these open-mouthed wailers,
these summer-camp slaughterers,
these *we have to go back*-ers.
Because they are us. Because
they are not. The frames churn.

IV.

I promise if our dog won't come in the house
we'll sell it, you say: insurance policy
for our technicolor doom.
There's a reason the asking price is low, you know?
We pore over and over the home invasions
and demonic toddlers drenched in gore, stunned
by the unbelievable trust—*maybe that moaning*
is only the wind. We won't make the same mistakes.
Then the layoff, the stillborn, or the poodle
mangled by the road won't slip between our ribs.
Or will it. Are there, finally, only endless
panoramas of grief. Kaleidoscopes
muddied, panes gone dark at the fringe.

V.

Now we know this much, at least:
If you hear a noise coming from the wardrobe,
run. If your wife tells you she's carrying
the devil's spawn, believe her. Leave the feral children
where you found them. When you exorcise evil,
it has to go somewhere. We understand it all, yes?
That when we bury our honey
under so many shovelfuls of soil,
if he comes back he'll never be the same.
His face we might recognize, its scar
on the left nostril, a pockmark cratering
the forehead like a test site. And yet—
that gleam in his eye: that's new.
We wait. We see what he'll do.

VI.

The theater is all clamor—
blaring its counsel, yelling to quiet
our protagonist's screams. The seats erupt
with strain, with worry, with popcorn and pain.
A flourbag-clad intruder idles
beyond her manicured reach. His chaos flits
like a songbird—her death hovers over her, wings
blackened and preened. When they slowly drive
the knife into her lover's side, she asks
the foolish question: the why.
Because you were home, he says.
Parrot with no pull string, she asks again.
How did she miss these lessons:
they do it because they can. Because
they're already there. Behind you.
Behind you. Behind you.

I Dream of Dick—He Dreams of a Woman in a Bottle

First
he was
her master,
then her husband.
For most women
it's the other
way
around. Horrid,
to think of it
now: at night
on Nickelodeon,
I roamed backward
black-and-white vistas,
enthralled. Mama let me watch
for hours unattended because
they were safe, or seemed it: the couples
in their separate twin beds. *Goodnight darling!*
Then nothing but a lampshaded *click*, the ottoman
always there to trip on like the truth: Lucy and Laura
and Samantha and Jeannie were so much smarter
than their men. My genie was so clever and kind, just
waiting for him on a Pacific beach. Her harem pants clean-
laundry-flapped: chiffon curtains in monochrome breeze
though the air was 60s stale inside that pink prison. My witch
was witty, could turn you into canned laughter or teeming
bestiary: parrot, poodle, chimp. Their husbands made
my women so small: insolent roommates, pert
girlfriends, each a plucky unwife. Everyone's name was
Dick. I can pretend that Nick at Nite was what
I called my boyfriend when he window-pebbled his way
inside our old blue house. But I spent nights wondering why
Samantha didn't turn that man into a canary and never look back.
How could she let him snuff her out? Was it a relief to cook a roast
instead of ruling the world? Can anyone hear me out there?

Kate Spade New York *Woodland Park*
Cat and Dog Salt & Pepper Shakers

Playful animal curiosities crafted of earthenware. Perfect for adding a dose of delight to any table.

Her name a nymph shell, a work of art, eclosed to reflect the woman and her worth. Surnames come and go, but empires are forever. Her handbags, tableware, and duvets: all ways to say *I've made it*. The beach-towel palette and got-my-shit-together snark drew me in—dots and dandelions seemed trendy again. *I'm from the Midwest, so I'm not much of a risk-taker*, she'd said. When I learn of her suicide, I smash the rest of the wedding china in the street.

*

That night, pacing the garden outside my Bensonhurst apartment, he said we didn't have anything left: *all we do is make cat jokes*. Before we owned the Shorthair I'd leave behind, we spoke a feline language all our own. I made a mistake, he took me back then didn't, and on and on in soap opera tones until there were only our words: *baby kitty, hissy, mew*. I thought their music was enough to save us. He took our words in vain; I saw the future was just a tiny vista, no wider than a cat door. I did not know this man. Our only plan for the future was to buy our kids a dog.

*

One of them is dark. One of them is light. One is a cat, the other a dog. One's fur is drawn on dark, the other's fur is scalloped in gold. The pepper has a single opening, just like the salt, though neither has ever been filled. One looks mean and the other looks nice. One looks trustworthy and the other damn suspicious. One has dotted eyes, can see what's in front of it. For years I thought one was blind. Then I opened my own eyes and saw what was there all along.

Jeopardy

I used to let you win sometimes
—did you know? When Trebek strode
on stage with his salvo of answers

> *Her poem "Lady Lazarus" ends, "Out of the ash*
> */ I rise with my red hair / And I eat men*
> *like air"*

you didn't hear me coo

> Who is Sylvia Plath

because I'd let those softballs whizz past
like logy bees, sluggish with honey,
arrested by sweetness as I was—

I thought sugar and silence were the same thing,

thought you'd love me if you could best me,
but I paid the cost of quiet.

> *His research study "Sexual Behavior*
> *in the Human Female" was a sensation*
> *in 1953*

It was never right between us,
not even when we shucked the clothes
from each other's bodies—

> Who is Alfred Kinsey

No, his clipboarded notes
would not have been kind: we were two lab rats
under glass, sparks singeing our paws.
My wedding dress was still fragrant with wine—

> *TLC describes this show with a rhyming title as*
> *"part fashion show, part bridal story, part*
> *family therapy"*

was it really so long ago
that you worried its pearl clasp?

What is *Say Yes to the Dress*

More like Say No, *am I right?*
you scold. But I'm already gone,
absorbed by the next answer:

> *This sister who inspired Eunice Shriver*
> *to found the Special Olympics died*
> *in 2005 at the age of 86*

That sweet sister who sang
"The Star-Spangled Banner" then stopped—

Who is Rosemary Kennedy

her acronymed *frères* pressed ether
into her: family secret. They sliced
until the human part was gone.

I *said*, who is Rosemary Kennedy

They made her small and I tried their trick
to make room for you: almond sliver,
dust mote, a pencil's shaved screed.

I tried, my love, to disappear

I said it. You didn't hear me?

You change the channel. I feel the pulse
of her cortex against the blade,
turn to ask you if you know

Hello?

that they quit cutting
when she quit singing, *oh, say.*

Cindy Crawford Home *San Francisco* Ash Rectangle Dining Table

With its clean lines and unusual materials, this table is a showstopper.

The woman who made the *All-American Girl* something other than the blonde-haired, blue-eyed nationalist dream first met with a plastic surgeon at 28: the same age I was married. Cindy's chili-pepper Versace gown is burned into our retinas; the piping-hot negligée that trussed me when I sprung from the cabin bathroom on my honeymoon cruise, however, failed to stop the show. The man I'd known for a decade kept watching *Jersey Boys* on a 12-inch TV. He fell asleep, the ribbons of my wrapping untouched. I fingered the spot above my lip where a dark mark should have been blooming.

*

Chrome and ash, modern to a fault: I had to have it then I had to get rid of it. The behemoth dwarfed each salon it tried. I helped a California college girl slide it into her father's old pickup. I waved goodbye. The meals we spilled on its pale veneer, the goodbye letters I drafted at its end—I hope the wood won't hold their heat. I hope our hands didn't stain it.

*

Eating in front of the television: the great American pastime. I wanted it to end, dreamt of him gazing at me across the table's width, through a candle's wriggling flame. The first night we owned it, I set our dinner on it, eye to eye. When I turned around, he'd set the plates beside one another. The Fiestaware dishes glared at me: a set of bloodshot eyes. *So we can see the TV*, he said. Every night after that we sat side-by-side, on the long edge, with nothing interrupting our view.

Love Meter

A few years from now, each cold night on the couch
will sound its rasping no. We won't hear it at first.

But today we're in San Francisco, wandering the wet,
uphill streets that meander like dreams—anthropologists

who tempt the lightning with an umbrella spoke, our shelter
a dripping carousel. We keep moving; we're still

in the same place. I visit Japantown in fog while you take meetings,
spending my little cash on ideas of animals cast in rubber—

erasers I line up on the railing outside, rank-and-file
as the seals we watch later, open-mouthed.

They, too, are made things, bulgebellies who slap
the wharf. I've been here before—this city of my last family

vacation, but this time you fill the grey streets
with your hailing. The cable cars that Mama loved

you derail with an errant hand, the cold drizzle halts
at the shore of your whitecapped smile.

These weeks are no different than the other three hundred
we've imbibed together, each slowly diluting my life

before you—the kaleidoscope of those who made me
dims and slows, even as I direct sequels

against the backdrops of those home videos—
me on the redwood roots,

Daddy piloting Mama in a wheelchair
I never imagined he'd push away.

We wind up at the arcade museum,
our bellies full of unlucky crab.

Each whirring antique dares us to forget
what's come before—

every morning we woke and agreed to stay,
our matching pillowcases a silent *yes*.

I can still see you dropping a quarter in as I watch
the firefly pop of the meter's bulbs

vacillating between TRUE LOVE and POOR FISH.
It's Valentine's Day, and last night you fell asleep

eating tuna tartare: I can't forget how little you cared.
You tighten your grip and we wait for the verdict—

how much easier to feed the machine our little choice?
My breath slows as the lights strike their pronouncements,

the tips of molten swords in blacksmith fire, revealing
a future your grip squeezes, steadily, towards.

Squeeze

Little girl cries. Little girl lets juice river the front of her dress.
Big girl watches, fondles a blood orange in grocery-store glare.

Little girl displeases her father. His eyes ripen; he dwarfs the shopping cart.
Big girl's veins ice over like back roads. Big girl knows what comes next.

Little girl's father squeezes her tiny hands in his: tight, tighter, tightest.
Big girl knows that pressure. Her once-husband's displeasure: a stolen necklace.

Little girl's mewling crescendos to scream: her fingers, pale petals scarlet with pain.
Big girl freezes. Big girl thinks her mother would know what to do.

Little girl shrieks, begs with her eyes: wet and brown as fruit rot.
Big girl's body hurls into their orbit. Big girl bellows: feathers come out instead of words.

Little girl is learning the yoke of men. Little girl's father wants to finish the lesson.
Big girl crushes the man with her stare. Big girl watches him let go her hands.

Little girl blubbers, wipes her splotched face. This lesson will not be her last. Big girl leaves the store, lights a cigarette with throbbing fingers.

Little girl glides down the aisle, a wounded bird. Her tears evaporate like rain. Big girl doesn't hold hands anymore. Big girl knows what hands can do.

After Eighteen Months of Marriage

for Jenny, after Dorianne Laux

I.

The day after the wedding we roamed
Ann Arbor in party garb. He listened
when I spoke. Sequins winked along
my waist, and it felt like a new life. I said
I'd always thought he was bad
at driving, and he agreed. All honesty
now possible, at least for a moment. He held
my hand. In the quiet of a cellar bar
he called it his paw, his little white biscuit.

Each day after that one was worse.
The fights, the breathless panic, the lies
and paperback sex. After eighteen months
it was over, but it felt like we'd been married
for just one frozen day. My magic
was used up; my fingertips sparked
but refused to light, denied us
their burst of rosewhite vim. I couldn't
make him happy; I couldn't even make dinner.
The hearth I once tended could only sigh
great breaths of cold snow.

II.

I return to the city where we met
and married, and every bricked façade
reminds me of him: the night
he hoodwinked a cop into believing
I was of age, the night he hoodslid
a whole block of cars in the new snow.
Like childhood toys and most
first kisses, he is more real in memory
than he ever was in life. Back then

I knew I was too young for love, but
fell in anyway. *Would you rather look*
at a thousand paintings for one second
or at one painting for a lifetime, I wrote
in a journal back then. I shove quarters
into the pinball machines that used
to dazzle us, remember his tight-lipped
kisses: perfunctory as a finger
pressed against a red button.

III.

I drink at our old haunts, douse
my debtor's heart.
He would take pleasure
in my pain if he knew: a little bird
crying *toldja so, toldja so.*
But I keep going. I love
and am loved again, wary
as a feral cat that comes inside.

Friends marry, and I am near:
what else to do but toast
and try? I noose the top pearl
of my best friend's ivory
gown, watch its tulle lift her
above herself. Alabaster bird,
little darling. She will leave him
in twenty-six days, and somehow
I already know. I grin and tell her
she is perfect—because we are
our mothers' daughters,
she smiles right back, a vision.

Waterford Crystal *Celebrations* Champagne Flutes

*Included in this exciting collection are six flute pairs,
including Love & Romance, Achievements, Anniversary,
Happy Celebrations, Believe, and Beginnings.*

The classic image of the champagne flute is not a single
glass, but a pair. Their rims touch, lip to singing lip, mid-
toast. Couples in the movies ivy-vine their arms as they
sip; the woman invariably titters, *the bubbles tickle my nose.*
Most of the time she is lying.

*

Don't get rid of them, Mama begged me after the split. So
far I've obeyed only because each one is worth just \$6
secondhand. No one wants to hex themselves, tippling
arsenic unawares. They lay, hull to hull, in the ocean-blue
sleep of their velvet box. She spent hundreds so I could be
like her. How can I tell her there's nothing to cheers. The
bubbles are carved right in: they don't need my help.

*

Like most objects, the flute has its critics. Some say it is not
expedient: the bouquet escapes into the air and disappears
(like most wives). It looks beautiful, but it is not practical
(like the tossing of the bouquet). Often top-heavy, it wants
to topple (like most institutions, like lies).

III.

"When a woman is eating with two men
she would naturally be seated between them…
A man eating with two women
would seat himself between them

unless one is his wife."

—*Ibid*

Layover

There was a mechanical bull and a waitress
who flirted with everyone. There was a rainbow
of cocktails served lukewarm in pint glasses,
two fingers of dread. We'd missed a flight
in bad weather but had been offered another.
There was only one seat. He wanted me
to get on, but I said no—wouldn't leave him.

Interred at a dark sports bar, we ended
the night eating wings cruelly torn
from an Atlanta-area buffalo. He watched
five games at once—linebackers creaming each other
in snow—and nothing was enough. Outside
I dialed a friend, asked her *is it weird he wanted me
to leave without him*? At the airport hotel

he laid his head on the sticky desk
in front of the mirror, defeated.
He was beside himself—
one version quite literally slumping
next to the other, and only one of them still
my husband. My eyes hurt from the obvious
overhead lighting. I asked him if he was okay
until I felt insane. We never know
how long we'll have to rest,
how long we'll nap in the terminal
of *not good enough* before we run,
out of breath, to board something better—

I wouldn't recognize myself
for years, had so far to go until
I could become a woman I'd want to know.

That night, there were gas station 40s and Cheetos.
There may have been pay-per-view porn.
Back home in Texas, Jolene may have been waiting
for his return: I couldn't hurry my knowing.
It was Christmas. When I opened
his gift, he whispered *next year*
and *better*. But there was no next year,
no better.

Scofflaw

The next morning, while countless grackles
machinate overhead, I bring my nose
to my shoulder and forearm, incline it
toward my bitten breasts. My skin

still smells like my lover. I carry his touch
in my cells as I stare, alone in predawn's
many-hearted thrum, at the back wheel
of my car, held fast with a metal boot.

A great word: these are the feet
that let me run from what I know
I must do—cook, clean, love only
one man at a time.

Love in the Time of World Literature Surveys

Poem beginning with a line by Kevin Prufer

Such sharp teeth. We were always hungry then.
We four fed each other, licking poems from our palms

to quell the tremors in our bellies, our brains.
On warm Texas nights when my heart

was large enough (which was most nights)
I carried you like children, held you, my lovers,

hands deep in your dirty hair. And in the morning
I stood before students with Ovid on my lips—

beg her to ratify a peace upon her bed—explaining that chaos
was the natural order, and marriage a mere oar

that slaps the sea's wild chop. I know havoc
fits me better than even the silk dresses you slid

from my shoulders each night. Tell me
you know the bedlam beneath the skin of my wrists—

where once my gnawed fingers grasped, an unclenched fist
now blooms: new narcissus. I'd had enough of holding on

and saw the shape of your struggle, could taste the want
that wetted your lips. And so I lifted mine to yours,

to breathe us new. *'Tis there that, all unarmed,
sweet concord dwells; 'tis there, the cradle of forgiveness,*

my tongue tells those thirty faces. But I do not tell them
that when we broke our fast, we saw the flash

of our icy teeth, our ravenous, hell-hot mouths.
We were starved. Are we starving still.

March Madness as Mamuralia

"On the Ides of March… a man clothed with
a goat-skin would be led in, and they would
strike him with long, slender rods, calling him
'Mamurius'… Mamurius himself was beaten
with rods and driven out of the city… [because]
difficulties had befallen the Romans."

—Johannes Lydus, *The Months* (*de Mensibus*)

It started with a fresh sports section, a paper
from the corner store. You loved the way I'd snap
open its leaf-thin folds, let it settle on my desk: clean sheets
on our marriage bed. I read up on ancient rivals, learned
each college town by name. The basketballs arced over
our screen, their suns setting and setting and setting.
Each team gripped by its own mythos;
each contest broke someone

                                    else's heart. Their sigils went on brawling
                    in my head: a Bulldog mauling a Gael, a Blue Devil
            fleeing a ravenous Wolverine. I loved you, and showed it
            by scanning the Sagarin ratings, the newspaper sunning
            its wings. We hung handwritten brackets on the freezer
            door, kept score in red and green ink. You loved to lose
            to me, pleased to have me in your world. We yelled
            at the referees, our bodies adjacent chapels, praying
                        for our teams alone—our fandom arbitrary
                    as the words for our foulness: *technical, flagrant,*

personal. I loved to make you happy; you didn't return
the favor. The books I'd stacked on your nightstand
were frosted with dust. You snoozed through readings
from the cheap seats while my spit anointed the mic.

Your games meant more than my poems; your games
meant more than me. Later I would dream of beating
a furred mascot with a stick, driving him from the arena.
You, the bearcat; you, the swing in my shoulder blade—
you, the bludgeoning bat.

The Marriage Bed

I hear they're putting Battaglia to death—
he killed his daughters while his wife listened
on the phone. I hear the news and think:

we humans are excellent at hurting each other.

You and I are two such scholars, capable
of limitless pain. Who sculpted us
into these forms, ever ready: *don't
patronize me,* or *go write a poem about it,* or

you're a drunk just like your father.

For years we slept like nested clothespins
in our twin-sized bed, our only relief
a broken futon that creaked and shuddered

like a rickety excuse.

These long weeks when we are fighting, the king
still isn't large enough. One of us retreats
to the couch—a private island of resentment, thin
as that old twin bed—to sleep away our anger,

or try.

Out there, alone, the clock glows green:
reproachful insect with a million
luminous eyes. When its glare proves too much,

we creep back to bed, the sheets grown cold on one side.

Somehow, we dream. And then, one night,
your hand reaches for mine in our big white bed.
It's always been there, warm and waiting, engraved
with the memory of every awful inch of me.

I've forgotten how to hold it.

Happy New Year

Year of too many keys on the key ring for too many not-my-houses / Year of my car's trunk choked with smoke-drunk clothes / You stopped kissing me on the mouth that year / Year of why is that bitch's handwriting on my chalk-boards & grocery lists / Your pantry swelled with potato chips that year because I was the one who cooked / Year of bar food & bar tabs & the bar closing / Year of moth bodies hurling themselves against strange windowpanes / More than once I slept on the driver's side when I came home & found the deadbolt thrown / Little year of ama-teur gemology so I wouldn't get screwed / Longer year of getting screwed nonetheless / I never had any money & always wanted to go home that year / I never knew what address to give / Year of spooning friends' mutts & sing-ing love songs into their blushing ears / Year of stroking sayonara into our cat's black stripes / That was the year of my feet's filthy bottoms because no one kept a house like I did / Year of not wanting to ever keep a house again / Year of taking down the photographs & swaddling them like suffocating babies / Yes the year every synonym for betrayal rimed my teeth / You said you fucked her out of grief / The year of losing face & remembering that I have a face / But let me yet utter another truth / That too was the year of god damn / I've never been happier than I am now / Yes that was the year of loving the permanence of stars / The year of whispering their frozen names

Instructions for Divorce

To leave for good, take out your tweezers.
In this fluorescent room, join your spouse: little word,
little blame bird, participle from the Latin, *to bind*.
Come with the vase of wedding sand

you poured together that day—your wash of blue
then her swath of green, you the shore and she the tide pulling you
out to sea, but together at least. Take the jar, gargoyle that once hulked
on the mantle: salt the ground with it. Spill the sage

and cerulean grains you matched to spring linens,
to bridesmaid dresses you've buried in closets,
burned through with naphthalene. In this sad sandbox, sit down.
Your husband's shirt is unironed. He reeks of another

woman's soap. There is much to be done. Your rings
glint under the fixtures like pinned beetles. Look closely:
pick your ceruleans from the clutch of her sages,
return your grains to your coffee cup. Your eyes will burn

with work, jeweler's loupes squeezed between your brows.
You'll smell her breath, that same perfume, the stray hairs haloing
her ears. No documents, no cruel crush of ink on paper, just the plink
of grains on glass. If you are quiet, you will hear them say,

think. The task is large—fault or folly, it all starts to look like the sea.
You might make it out of this place: two ruins. Or you'll fill a bucket,
its bottom pegged like a turret's top. Go, tip it over:
a careful stab, a castle's breathless keep.

Encomium in Which I Cannot Be Contained

I learn of an octopus who escaped
the little diorama of the sea

in which he'd been interned. Crafty
bastard: his eight legs slurped

into a drainpipe that emptied him
into the ocean. What a wonder—

not content to be mere
decoration, mere idea, Inky

Shawshanked out of the aquarium,
crept beautifully back

to his first context, unlike the stasis
of the cube where I beheld Hirst's shark

for the first time, years ago. Nothing
could quell my terror in the face

of its open mouth—I was gripped
by some instinct to get the hell

out of the way. Its silent mass of fins
still floats in the city,

limpid in watercolor, like the blue
phosphenes that skate

inside my eyelids. Up close
the shark's artifice is clearer—

something's lost in the piercings
that suspend its bulk aloft:

like a slip showing, like a scarred
set of breasts. But still the black gape

of its jaws, womb-like and serene.
Still the artist's muted murder

flickering in the cube. But the shark
itself seemed more void than being:

the octopus in the exhibit exists, the dead
shark under glass does not.

In absence, you see, the mind
makes presence: press on your eyes

and a prisoner's cinema
blooms: unwanted anemone,

in this cell like any other.
I never had more

than when I had nothing in that city:
no money and countless dreams.

Bars on the windows and rats
in the kitchen, robberies

in broad daylight, pink slips
and overdrawn bank accounts.

Will you listen if I tell you
I have been an octopus, all tendril

and grasp, my want
unstoppable. But I want you

to know one thing, the truth's
frigid tide as it comes in:

the ocean is a tank
too, just bigger.

Unsolicited

The song goes *We are sentimental slaves on broken knees.* My therapist goes *the stones stretch back endlessly*, so far that no one can claim to have cast the first. Mama goes *marriage isn't always fun.* My dentist goes *you need to floss more*, to snap your dregs from between my teeth. My mentor goes *you're at the height of your powers*, calls it the divorce bump. My landlord goes *the rent's past due again.* My friend goes *stay here as long as you need.* My lover goes *I didn't know but I've always dreamed of your mouth.* The other woman just sits there, a snake with its venom squeezed out. The song goes *Love has taken us as far as we can reach.* My husband goes *I never paid attention to the lyrics.* My phone goes *beep*, tells me that last year I wrote them on my hand. I go dark like ocean deep, craving the old way, then shuck off its call like a shell.

I Am Because We Were

This is the one where I try to love the way he'd fall asleep
at parties, or the way he'd smell his hand after jamming it

into his cargo shorts. He played video games fifty hours
a week while I earned degrees, kept house, threw the best

& most raucous parties. What did he offer me, beyond a lonely
decade? I stroke the hair of my young self, say *every error*

has brought you here. But he could be funny & sometimes kind:
rubbed ice on my back when I shook with fever, played the Gomez

to my Morticia. At our rehearsal dinner I gave him a dread-heavy watch
inscribed with the continents, said *I want to see the world with you*

& somehow knew I wouldn't. It turns out good marriage is like
good business: partnerships last when they're mutually beneficial.

Our terms became unfavorable, soaked with her knockoff perfume.
But like everyone else, we did what we were supposed to do: we tried

to make life's gall taste sweeter. I remember that first summer—we ate
only Panchero's & jammed to Peter Bjorn and John on the drive

to Traverse City. His old yellow lab bared her teeth at me, a warning
I ought to have heeded. But he frisbeed me a slice of bologna,

helped me learn to appease her instead. That year I stood
at his mother's grave, cleared its weeds, plucked those that flowered

& put them in her pot. He didn't cry or say a word. I learn the term
in an article I edit for extra cash two summers after I leave him,

broke but wonderfully free: *ubuntu.* There was love there, once—
I take that to bed like a lover thought lost at sea. I am because

we are, somewhere, still out there, half-buried at West End Beach,
him taking my picture & saying *you look like a mermaid,*

me leaning back, long hair snapping in the wind, saying *don't
get my cigarette in the shot*—keeping the uglier truths out of frame.

IV.

"Glance at the hostess and adopt her method whenever in doubt as to what to do."

—*Ibid*

After the Party at the Bad Love Museum

Watch your step—haven't swept up yet.
Every night, we throw a party so the installations
won't be lonely. Life imitating art and all that. To your left,

> **People Are Staring**
> 2015
> Plastic, human finger,
> audio recording
> 47.9865.1

you'll see a working telephone
you can press to your very own ear. Dial 5
to hear him shush me in public again
and again: a dumb ocean on the other end,

and over here you'll see a vintage bridal veil
fastened to a she-wolf in heat. Keep your hands
inside the bars, please. She doesn't
like visitors. There's much to see.

No flash, please. Careful, someone
spilledtheir prosecco just here.
A question?

> **First-Look Photos**
> 2014
> Silk chiffon, canis
> lupus, glass, steel
> 60.198511.2

Yes, in the gift shop
you can purchase a copy of the game
he played from sun to moon
and would return to after dinner, after sex,
you know. The one where little monsters
slaughter each other with axes. Such fun—

> **The Way to a Man's Heart**
> 2014
> Ink, tallow, linen
> 57.198409.5

abuse, yes, but some have accused me
of sarcasm. Did you know the word
comes from the Greek *sarkazein*, to tear
the flesh? Which reminds me,

if you're hungry, have a look at the weekly menus
I used to tape to the fridge like good proof: see
how useful I was. Scallops Provençal on weeknights,
perfectly portioned to help us lose weight.

I could tell you how we got thin together then welded
our lives into the metal casts our parents made. How,
newly confident, he fucked a woman whose obvious beauty

could only be a weapon, but
a dull one—a plastic knife
plucked from the trash.

> **Friendsgiving**
> 2015
> Vodka, butter, human
> tongue, fish hook
> 9.66613.07

I was always best at a party. You should have seen me
last night, swirling about with trays of hors d'oeuvres.

I made the cocktails we drank the night he lured me
into an orgy. Mashed potato martinis: I could taste
the cube of frozen butter on her tongue when we
all fucked each other and no one enjoyed it a bit.

The music last night—you should have heard it.
Carnegie acoustics in the main hall!
The silence was always the worst…
the thing he was best at, you know.
Over here you can listen: if you're patient,
you can make out the chandelier sound
of the keys I threw when he asked why
I bother writing when it doesn't make a dime.

> **Untitled (Silence)**
> 2016
> Shadow box, tin can,
> cotton string
> 88.9543.44

Mmm. We like our women artists nude, yes? On canvas
and off? Vulnerable, from the Latin *vulnerare*, of course,
to wound. And that's what you're really here to see.
But it's not so much *bad man hurt me* because
this is not about bad man, this is about why we choose
little men who try to make us small too, about *bad* and *men*

and *marriage* and world of men,
whirlpool of men, of hoping… pardon me…
our daughters might do better. But let me tell you,

the road map is unclear, muddied
with thumbprints and cheap wine.
You try to love a man, to do it better
than Mama, only to make yourself a crumb.

I should have grown fat
on myself instead of starving
into that dress. To resell one,
you see, you do best to show it
wrapped around a body,

tissue paper buttressing
every false curve. When the reception
is over and the marriage ends, this presents
a particular dilemma—

hold my drink? I have to pee. See that fountain? Once,
Mama's basement flooded—water poured from the ceiling
onto her old wedding gown and mine, entombed
in their white boxes, twins buried in the same cemetery.
When I laughed at the sight of them, she screamed.

Maintenance
2012
grass, tobacco, gouache,
underwire, bile on cowhide
8.1923.1

Sunk Cost Fallacy
ca. 2005–2016
flower, hummingbird egg,
lard, sugar, saline, breastmilk,
baking soda, menstrual blood,
wax, ash
9.8504.7

They're here, you know: let's see them—
just this way, past those bruised watercolors
of the night he held down my arms (oh yes)
and the birthday cakes (eleven!) rotting
in those wondrous cases.

We'll come back to them later. We have all
the time in the world. Don't you know? This place
never closes. Truly! Not even on Christmas Day.

But here: here they are. Haunting,
no? Of course, you may wonder,
couldn't a child have done this?
And that is, in part, the point.
What else is there to say, in the end,
about paintings that won't be held
by their frames?

Family Plots
2018
Silk, taffeta, water, Perspex,
acrylic paint, soil, granite
10.1236.4

V.

"They rise, he helps her with her coat or other impedimenta and leads the way out of the dining room."

—*Ibid*

Happy Birthday

for T. again, and always—December 5, 2019

And back in Texas you are ripped clean
from the old life: we not-getting-any-
younger women with unfrozen eggs,
washing down chèvre with merlot, pretending
to know what kind of women we wanted
to be. So far our answer is *the kind who are loved*
without labor. But all love

is labor; you would know. There is a new baby
warming itself on your chest, where we once dripped
hot wax between each others' breasts, adorned
ourselves with rose petals, the grave dirt of poets
who might have used our bodies for pleasures
less noble than children. And now you are a child
again as you hold your new life: I pray the envy
out of my bones. At your shower, you played
Rosemary, threatened your bump
with a knife. The year was one, and I never
loved you more. It's your birthday, too, moon

goddess maiden-come-mother. If we burned
each other with the fires of want back then,
from third-coast snow let me warm you, belly fed
by your creation: a reed through which much music
will flow. My sister, we're the ones who love
ourselves best. Thank you for this twanging song—
the sound of an arrow racing forward
into all that unknown air.

Order Following Hearing on Petition to Change Name

STATE OF MICHIGAN   FILE NO. ███████
Judicial Circuit – Family Division

In the matter of the name change of ████████████

The old one was a homophone for *what came before*
and that seemed clever for a while. *No woman's
name is hers*, I muttered, lying alone at night. *At least*

THE COURT FINDS:

it will be the last one I take. My maiden name
reminds me of my bullies and my father's: I can see them
holding him, screaming *here cow, eat some grass.*

At least I got to choose, I'd whisper while signing
a check. This name was already mine, and seemed unlikely
to leave me. Easy to spell when ordering lattés—

3. Notice of hearing was given by publication

it was a trochee like my other name. I didn't want to sign
another paper that slurred *it's over.* No one could trace
my history to the hilt, I thought: a scorpion inside

a cave of my own making. One night I dreamt of giving it away
like an old coat, like the daughter we never had. *I won't have
to buy new business cards*, I said, tossing my head.

7. The request for the name change of ████████████
     □ is   ☑ is not   made with fraudulent intent

My laugh lifted from a 90s movie. I was like my mother, worrying the name of what she'd lost in her pocket like a stone. I was sure I could be a new person with the same face, carve the past into

my future like a drunk tattoo. I had to prove I would stay in some forsaken way the same. But it is my name. I drum my chest with dirty hands—*I cannot have another in my life.*

□ 13. The name(s) of the following person(s) is/are changed

You see, I've been so many women. Let the snail shell of my name labyrinth me back to life. I gave a man my soul, and left him as I found him, thank god: with the cry of his only name.

▌▌▌▌▌▌▌▌▌▌▌▌   ▌▌▌▌▌▌▌▌▌▌▌▌

Date   Judge

What Stillness Is

for Trista

"Faintings 110; shrieks 20 (per performance); left theater (first act 19); left theater (second act) 150, left theater (third act) 1; returned (after revival) 100; returned visit 10 (per performance); husbands summoned to escort home wives 10 (per performance); taxicab increase 500%"

—Dracula's first seven weeks at the Biltmore Theater,
L.A. Times, August 1928

In the theater the women faint   we've been at it for years   our collapsing   & quaking our

crumpling at blood & bile   But I've done one better: I faint & they gild   my pockets

I know what stillness is   my sisters too   this our sole inheritance this   our heart's white

desert   You know the scene: woman alone   in the kitchen woman   alone

at her needlework woman alone   eyes rolled to snowdrift—heart slowing   slowed   I will be your

nothing; I already am   Your empty post-show glow your canary   in a coffin: its only song

the quiet   of an angry husband's house I am   the greatest fainting   woman in the world

this is no act You see   we slip out of time: our tiny black escapes   & then back in: we bleed   to

life before the Count's empty reflection   He is not there; that is   his terror & ours   now Lugosi

feasts on Lucy   his endless thirst unslaked until   a man unsheathes his favorite weapon

The whalebone sucks   our skinny
of breath & power—   my faint is no
turned to smoke like my sisters long ago
the monster it births   Fear what's born from
This is my house & I'm on the floor   my pain sells tickets
remember every evil   is born
Without us is no us   so bring
honey   I've got bills to pay

impaling the creature   he stuffs the shiv inside him deep
ribs   squeezes my sisters to exhaustion   but I am full
fear   I got paid while they burned him & his film
Do not fear the stillness—   the closed casket &
the quiet   womb before the storm
puts asses in seats   When you turn out the lights
of woman   I don't have to kill you; you're   already dead
the smelling salts Watch me   drink the darkness

Jobs I Am Willing to Do If They Mean Getting Free of You

will I soak will I
sanitize & shitscrub
will I ache
in the balls of my feet
will I manage the night
shift at a Steak 'n
Shake in Texarkana
Texas will you

hire me hate
me hurl
epithets
when I forget
to lock the sticky
door on a loony
June night in the blue
back of a walk-
in freezer
at a forgotten
Save-a-Lot in Maine

yes to all yes
to the trim bank
account the coins
pitched like insults yes
to the plastic
smile of a name
placard a pin
stabbed in the flesh
that guards
my penniless heart

some young
wife will eye
me as she cups
the change
I spill into her
hand like alms

when she gets
home the frozen
roast will hold
my fingerprints
she'll leave
it she'll leave
him & everything
will taste of grass
someday
she'll mow
one ordinary
afternoon herself

Happy Mother's Day

"The truth is, much of what we have traditionally
believed about babies is false. We have misunderstood
and underestimated their abilities. They are not simple
beings but complex and ageless—small creatures with
unexpectedly large thoughts."
—David Chamberlain, *The Mind of Your Newborn Baby*

I never moved toward the light. In a hospital
in downtown Detroit, they lifted me
from you, flashed my crone's face
over the drape, then pushed me away
in a box. Stitches

ripping, you found me—
said my name for the first time. Some say
we choose our parents, watch a cosmic
film of what's to come then slam
our spark into our mother's wombs. Oh Mama,

my sun slowly cooling, always
in the same place. Did I choose you? Am I here
only as umbra? I dream you'll lift yourself
from bed with my hands, wheel down
the tiled wing, find your own body

swaddled in a cart. I am your lesson,
love's swollen allure. We crawl toward
the ocean's lip. The salt is bad
for our hearts.

Lord Don't Let My Heart Be Weak

Not enough blood, she says
How can that be, I say
Inverted waves, she says
I've always been unique, I say
You mean alone, she says
No, I say
They're like green valleys, she says
Yes, I say
You're sitting too much, she says
Papers to grade, I say
Walk and talk, she says
Poems, I say
Weld them into the air, she says
Lay down in the green valley, I say
The greenest, she says
Not yet, I say
No, not yet, she says

Instructions for Divorce

This is how to do it.

First, see if you recognize yourself
in photographs.

Then cut your hair.

Tell yourself it's time
for another change. Don't wonder
about what kind.

Stay up late treading water.

Fall asleep on a friend's couch. Wait
for the accusation.

Tell him you weren't in his bed.

Read a book about two poets
lying head to toe, reading.

Grieve this image.

Go on dawn hikes with booze
still whispering through your veins.

Tell the girl who smells it on your skin
she doesn't know how hard
the rain can fall.

Fly back to your husband.

Worry about
his new goatee.

Wonder if it makes him look
like a villain. Decide
it does. Say nothing.
Lose your breath.

Feel it fill you again
in the mouth of another man.

Don't kid yourself—Laurie
was no good for Jo.

Have panic attacks. Ask for help.

See that you were two children playing
their parents' sorry games.

Don't move back home.

Pray to the redheaded wick
of every candle in the house.
Burn each one.

Ask yourself if you can live
without the stacks of good china.
Smash them.

Cry one night for every sequin
on that dress.

Know that there's no manual
for this. Then write one.

Think about detachment
then weld yourself
to the world's blue ache.

Look again.

To My Little Self

Remember the cookies   just two or three

castled in the little glass   dish glinting in Michigan's sorry

excuse for sun   you were seven and went back

for more   two or three   when Mama came back

from the deck she scolded   what   was it that she said

does it matter   what matters is that you waited at the kitchen

counter for an hour after she went back   outside the sky

slowly darkening   you would not   disappoint her no

you were seven years old   if you did not eat them you

were good   you would make her see you were good

I'm here to tell you to eat them   and everything else

life will offer   the bitter men and sweet

distractions to come   eat it all   none of it matters

you will never be good   you do not have to be good

one day that tattoo will grace the skin   behind your clavicle

your little black   rebellion   it got so dark

that Mama came back inside   saw the bowl

the untouched wafers   said   what did she say

what matters is that she chided you   again you had

fucked up   it's ok   we can say that now

the earth spun the sad   Midwestern sky to sludge and you

have never forgotten that day even   as your waistline surged

and ebbed   a fleshy tide   you will never be able to harness

it's ok   I'm here to tell you there are larger wrongs and you

will commit them all devour   them all and life will go on

the world   will keep on spinning

the sun neither rises nor sets it's just you   baby girl

turning   and turning

Happy Birthday

> "I am thinking that a poem could go on forever."
>
> —Jack Spicer

Tell me the story of the night I was born.

Mama's palm is on her laboring back, shopping for china.

This is an origin story, like the half-tale she tells, in a dress I imagine was red.

I'm as old as she was, and stayed up until five last night, waiting for Radiohead tickets.

I slept guiltily, woke to find them gone. I resolved to shed all numbers.

The warm sigh of our bed has whiskey on its breath.

Tell me if I will ever use *love* in a poem and be able to mean it.

Instead I'll mention the two gray hairs I dreamt of culling from your nape.

The shears cut like moonlight, the mouth lets fall its own name.

Tell me why I can't stop thinking about the city I loved so much I left it.

Now it's entrusted to women who waste their baby names on protagonists.

I have no use for imagined children: a string of light bulbs fighting.

You question the width of my neck; it still turns towards the lichened reservoirs.

Against an aquarium sky I count my fingers like my mother did, bleary through morphine eyes.

This poem is about the creature that swallowed ⅓ of my pie.

The hope is that one day the highway lights will spell something out in Morse code just for me.

What is the difference between an urban backdrop and a picture taken in the city?

The photographed remain and disappear, eyes flat, glimmering, here and no place else.

Schrödinger used a cat, but to me there's no point unless it's an infant.

All my life I have been chasing the *gestalt* of a bend in the woods of Charlevoix, Michigan.

On my 39th birthday I will write a contrite poem about the child I bore and named Worry.

By then I will have given up on sestinas, the possibility of God, the wind that eats my kites.

The last thing I'll write is an account of the long year when death made a home in my eyes.

I was sixteen, and I don't think I've ever made it farther.

Three decades of holding vigil for the houseguest who always comes.

I'm my own unruly golden dog.

One Year Later, I See *The Two Fridas* in Dallas

and think   this is the two-heartedness of divorce
there is no way   in 1939   Kahlo was not thinking of before
and after   the bloody sewing that must
be done if one   is to get away   to become another
to transcend the vestments   that starch her skin
to become her own second thought
who made these rules   there are no rules
I signed the papers this time last year   happy anniversary
had to read aloud   *my marriage is destroyed*   his Hyde
showed up that day   *that's what you've got to say* he chided
he seemed sure   I wouldn't say it   that I couldn't
bring myself   to demolition   he snorted shade
from his nostrils   I knew that side well   but he   was no bull
I slid off his back before   he could fling
my weight against the wall   lucky for me   my best twin
showed up that day   she don't give a shit about shame
I want more   I shouldn't have it   or should I
there were two of him   and only   one ever said *yes*
I took forceps and clamped   the vein between
the phantom I'd become   and the woman still kicking
my ribs inside   this time last year   I wrote *you cannot*
simply go on   *the same woman you once were*
there are   of course   other interpretations
for instance   did you know the word *hostess*
used to mean *stranger*   a kind of guest at her own party
you're no longer a guest in your own body
I tell myself   a little parting gift

I Watch Myself on TV

even though it's not me there. I have to admire
the untamed woman sewn into a dress

that didn't fit, can't help but watch her—
the wrong Ken doll embalmed at the end

of the aisle. But I root for her anyway, laugh
when I'm supposed to: the groom cracks

a joke only funny to him. I don't judge.
She is becoming—she is her own

first bloom. She leaves him &
I cheer. She falls in love with a heel

& I like him though I shouldn't, cry
when she crawls into the bathtub

while he makes dinner, cradling
a chef's knife to her ribs. I never change

the channel & the show
is always on. I've seen it so many times

I mouth the lines by heart. Her mother says
you weren't the easiest child, & I know

they're in the car midway through
the worst season, speeding

down 96 in the dark. Her not-husband
says *I don't believe you* when she tells him

she's been faithful—I can almost smell
the gin & glass-sweat on his palms.

When she eats cheesecake, I don't worry
she'll get fat: she is Aphrodite

with hair undone & fork in hand.
What I mean is, everything

is forgiven. Every man whose lips
she'll forget, every fucked star

that eyeballs her stumble
back home: it's miracles

all the way down. The time slot
is *always*. I binge her, I am her.

I'll love the ending even if it's predictable,
& I'll always want a season more. So will she.

But she'll get some of it—the applause
wild, the stars like confetti.

Acknowledgments

These poems have appeared in the following journals—some under different titles, in earlier versions, or under a different name. Many thanks to the editors and readers who believed in my work and helped it reach a wider audience:

bad pony: "What Stillness Is"

Barstow & Grand: "Happy Birthday"

Blue Earth Review: "Happy New Year"

Cold Mountain Review: "Instructions for Divorce"

DEAR Poetry Journal: "Jeopardy"

Denver Quarterly: "Cindy Crawford Home *San Francisco* Ash Rectangle Dining Table," "Kate Spade New York *Woodland Park* Cat and Dog Salt & Pepper Shakers"

Gulf Coast: "Happy Birthday"

Midwestern Gothic: "What's Left of Michigan"

The Mississippi Review: "Half Past"

The Missouri Review: "Eating Alone"

New Ohio Review: "Layover"

Nightjar Review: "Self-Portrait as Maillard Reaction"

Nimrod: "Best Order"

Passages North: "Waterford Crystal *Celebrations* Champagne Flutes"

Pleiades: "Happy Halloween"
Public Pool: "Squeeze"
Rogue Agent: "To My Little Self"
Spiderweb Salon: "March Madness as Mamuralia"
Southword: "Love Meter"
Tinderbox Poetry Journal: "Folie à Famille"
Up North Lit: "Happy Everything"

Thank you to my dear friend, most trusted reader, and unofficial agent Jenny Molberg. Where would I be without your fine eye and ear? Without your warmth and spark and enormous heart?

To the countless friends and fellow poets who read these poems and this manuscript and urged me on during the years I spent working on it, especially Heidi Kaloustian, Carly Kaloustian, Katie Watts, Bess Whitby, Trista Edwards, Ashley Reis, Jessi Lauffer, and Matt Miller: your friendship and your belief in me and in my work have kept me afloat even in times of hardship and disbelief. Thank you.

Thank you to mentors Morgan LaRocca and Thierry Kehou, and the entire *Poets & Writers* Get the Word Out cohort: Dimitri Reyes, Sahar Muradi, Ashia Ajani, Ae Hee Lee, Leslie Sainz, Jorell Watkins, Sebastian Merrill, Olatunde Osinaike, and Violet Spurlock. Learning from you and alongside you has been an incredible honor.

Thank you to the sublime Diane Seuss, whose words of wisdom have affected my writing and my life as a writer so deeply. Having your support for this work is an honor I could scarcely have dreamed of when I first put this manuscript together.

I'd like to thank B. H. Fairchild, Bruce Bond, Corey Marks, Mark Bibbins, David Lehman, Robert Polito, and Ken Mikolowski, who helped me see that my deepest education would be the one I embarked on myself after earning my graduate degrees.

Thank you to Meghan O'Rourke, Laurie Sheck, and Mary Jo Salter: I have long treasured your words of encouragement.

I want to express my gratitude for the time, space, and creative freedom I was afforded by the Sewanee Writers' Conference and the Hambidge Center for Creative Arts. Residing with you changed my life in tangible and inspiring ways, and directly enabled the completion of this book.

Thank you to Dr. Ross Tangedal, Cornerstone Press, and my fellow Portage Poetry Series pressmates. Your support for this work has changed everything.

Thank you to my colleagues at Blue Lake Fine Arts Camp both at home and abroad: doing this deeply good work alongside you has helped to nurture my creative and personal life in countless ways.

Many thanks to Dr. Charles Blankson, whose scholarship I learn so much from. Your patronage and continued support of my work has immensely benefited me for a decade. "I Am Because We Are" owes its existence to our work together.

Mom and Peep: you've given me everything. The rest is just icing on the cake. Thank you.

Most of all, thank you to my husband, John Schonbok. This book is a reckoning with all that came before you, and your entrance into my life has only thrown the past into starker relief. No one was surer that this book would be born than you, and I'm awed by the fact that I get to be on your team forever. I love you.

Lastly, thank you to my daughter, Matilda. Thank you for choosing me to be your mama. I signed the contract for this book on your due date. You are made of magic as a love letter to the future, like all good poems are. May it all get even better from here. I've got you, baby girl.

Notes

"Folie à Famille"

Rachel Aviv's article about *uppgivenhetsydrom*, a disorder observed in Swedish children who are clinically healthy but have fallen into comas after being scheduled for deportation, gives the poem its epigraph. (Aviv, Rachel. "The Trauma of Facing Deportation." *The New Yorker*, 27 March 2017: newyorker.com/magazine/2017/04/03/the-trauma-of-facing-deportation.)

"Happy Birthday"

The poem's epigraph is the last line from Jack Spicer's "Psychoanalysis: An Elegy" (Spicer, Jack. *My Vocabulary Did This to Me: The Collected Poetry of Jack Spicer*. Wesleyan University Press, 2010).

"I Am Because We Were"

The poem's title is a play on the translation of the word *ubuntu*, an African philosophy which emphasizes humanity toward others. This Nguni Bantu term is often translated as "I am because we are." The epigraph comes from a work of scholarship that considers the marketing implications of economics in cultures who hold this philosophy dear. "As in marriage, the partners agree to exchange with each other, unless the terms of the partnership become unfavorable," the authors write. My gratitude to Dr. Charles Blankson for allowing me to excerpt it here after working on it many years ago as an editor. (Elliot, Blankson, Ngugi, & Glassburner, "Leveraging Ubuntu to Enhance Positioning Activities in B2B Markets in Sub-Saharan Africa.")

"Jeopardy"

> The *Jeopardy* questions quoted were taken from the online J! Archive files for Show #7222, aired on Tuesday, January 26, 2016; Show #5124, aired on Thursday, December 14, 2006; and Show #7321, aired on Monday, June 13, 2016. The poem also refers to the 1941 lobotomy of Rosemary Kennedy, sister of John F. Kennedy. I also had in mind a poem (which contains the line "see you can say oh") by Ken Mikolowski, my professor and mentor at The University of Michigan, as I contemplated the fact that the doctors performing the lobotomy asked Rosemary to sing familiar tunes like the national anthem in order to judge when they had successfully cut the connections in her prefrontal cortex: the locus of human abstraction, social behavior, and personality.

"March Madness as Mamuralia"

> The poem's epigraph is taken from Johannes Lydus' *De Mensibus*, a text about the months of the Roman calendar and their attendant rituals. (Lydus, John. *On the Months [De Mensibus]* Trans. Anastasius C. Bandy,

Eds. Anastasia Bandy, Demetrios J. Constantelos, and Craig J. N. de Paulo. Lampeter: Edwin Mellen Press, 2013.)

"Order Following Hearing on Petition to Change Name."

The lines "But it is my name. I drum / my chest with dirty hands—*I cannot have another in my life.*" are derieved from similar lines in Arthur Miller's *The Crucible* (1953).

"Unsolicited"

The song lyric quoted in the first line is from Zedd's "Addicted to a Memory" (Zaslavski, Anton. *True Colors*, Interscope Records, 2015, Track 1).

Other

The collection's epigraph appears in Chapter 35 of Louisa May Alcott's *Little Women*.

The book's section epigraphs are lifted from *Practical Cookery and the Etiquette and Service of the Table: A Compilation of Principles of Cookery and Recipes with Suggestions for Etiquette for Various Occasions.* (1st ed., Department of Food Economics and Nutrition, School of Home Economics, Kansas State College of Agriculture and Applied Science. John Wiley & Sons, 1947.)

CAITLIN COWAN lives on Michigan's west coast with her husband, their young daughter, and two mischievous cats. Her poetry, fiction, and nonfiction have appeared in *Best New Poets, The Rumpus, New Ohio Review, Missouri Review, Southeast Review, Denver Quarterly, SmokeLong Quarterly, The Account,* and elsewhere. A Pushcart and Best of the Net nominee, Caitlin has won the Littoral Press Poetry Prize, the Mississippi Review Prize, and an Avery Hopwood Award. Ilya Kaminsky also selected her poem, "Flight Plan," to win the Ron McFarland Prize for Poetry. Her work has received support from the Hambidge Center for Creative Arts, the Sewanee Writers' Conference, and the Vermont Studio Center. Caitlin holds degrees from the University of North Texas, The New School, and the University of Michigan. She has taught writing at UNT, Texas Woman's University, and Interlochen Center for the Arts. Caitlin works in arts nonprofit administration for Blue Lake Fine Arts Camp, where she serves as Director of International Programs and as Chair of Creative Writing. Caitlin also serves as a Poetry Editor at *Pleiades* and writes *PopPoetry,* a weekly poetry and pop culture newsletter. Find her at caitlincowan.com.